15 Tips For A Stronger Marriage

Practical Tips For Newlyweds, Nearly-Weds Or Anyone Who Wants To Strengthen Their Marriage

ERIC ELDER

INTRODUCTION
by Eric Elder

I was sitting with a couple recently to help them plan their wedding when the bride-to-be asked me to do something impossible: she wanted me to talk at her wedding about marriage and what made my marriage to my wife, Lana, so successful.

She said she admired our relationship and wanted to learn whatever she could to make her marriage the best that it could be.

Here's why her request seemed so impossible: how could I possibly summarize 23 years worth of thoughts on marriage in such a short message on her wedding day? Yet her question also inspired me because I loved the idea of being able to pass along to them anything that might be helpful. So I began to think of all the tips I had heard before we got married, after we got married and throughout our 23 years of marriage. I quickly came up with 4 or 5 sermons to share at her wedding!

In the end, I only shared 1 simple message with them, based on 3 words, which I felt would help them get through anything they might face in the future. I'll share those 3 words with you in chapter 6, as they serve as the glue that holds all the other tips together. But I still wanted to share with this couple all the other great tips that God had brought to my mind. The result is this little book that I'm now sharing with you.

I wish I could say that if you'll just put these 15 tips into practice you'll be guaranteed success in your own marriage, but relationships just don't work like that. Each one of us is unique and each one of our relationships is unique. Yet I still believe each of these tips can be helpful to you in one way or another, even if it's just to talk through them with your spouse, or spouse to be, and then adapt and apply them to your own relationship.

To make this book easier to read, I've divided it into 7 chapters, 6 of which are about marriage, with a bonus chapter at the end called "12 Tips On Parenting." I wrote this chapter in response to another question by some other friends who asked for my thoughts on that topic.

Since this book has 7 chapters, you might want to read a chapter a day for 7 days or a chapter a week for 7 weeks. You might also want to go through this book with a few other couples who are newly married, nearly married or just want to strengthen their marriage, no matter how long they've been married. Who knows? This book may be just what they need to make their marriage not just good, but great!

Any way you do it, I pray God will bless you through it, both now and for many years to come.

In Christ's love,
Eric Elder

CHAPTER 1

Here are the first 7 tips for a stronger marriage. I've kept these tips short to help you get started as quickly as possible, but I hope you won't rush through them.

We have a game at our house called *Othello.* and the description on the box says the game takes "a minute to learn; a lifetime to master." The same is true for each of these tips. You can probably read each one in just a few minutes, but they could take a lifetime to master!

So I hope you'll take some time to really consider how to apply each one to your own marriage. With that in mind, here are the first 7 tips!

1) Pray with each other daily. Before Lana and I got married, I heard someone say that he prayed every night with his wife before they went to bed. He said this assured them of 2 things every day:

1) This assured them that each of them was being prayed for every single day of their lives. Since I believe in the power of prayer, I was so eager to try this even before I got married that I tried it with a friend who was my roommate at the time. It turned out to be so powerful, and we saw so many answers to our prayers, that I was convinced to keep doing it when I entered into marriage as well.

2) This also assured them that each of them would have a chance to express some of their deepest needs that they may never have shared otherwise. Often I would go through a whole day with Lana, talking and doing life together, and think that I knew what she probably wanted prayer for by the end of the day. But there were often times when I would ask her how I could pray for her and she would surprise me with something that I would have never guessed on my own.

No matter how late it was at night or what kind of mood we were in, we kept this commitment daily, even if it was just praying a blessing over each other in Jesus' name. One of Lana's favorite prayers to pray for me and for the kids was based on this verse from the Bible:

"The LORD bless you and keep you; the LORD make His face shine upon you and be gracious to you; the LORD turn His face toward you and give you peace" (Numbers 6:24-26).

I shared this tip with the couple who inspired me to write this book and they posted a message on FaceBook just a few days into their honeymoon:

"A man filled with great wisdom told us before we got married that every night we should pray together before we fell asleep. So far in our short marriage we have done that. There is nothing more intimate."

I agree! Pray with each other every day.

2) Take out the TV. Lack of communication is the #1 cause of divorce. It's amazing how even *having* a TV in the room can impact your communication with your spouse. It's always easier to turn on the TV than to talk to someone else. The TV doesn't talk back; you don't have to listen if you don't want to. You can be delighted and entertained for hours on end without doing any of the heavy lifting of a relationship. Having a TV in the room is like always having a third person in your marriage. Even when it's off, the temptation is still there to turn it on.

Lana and I read a book before we got married called *The First Years of Forever* by Ed and Gaye Wheat which argued convincingly that the patterns you set in the first 2 years of marriage will set the tone for the patterns you'll have in your 7th year and 14th year and so on. So to set your patterns right from the start, make communication a #1 goal. Lana and I put our TV in the back of a closet for the first year of our marriage. The only time we took it out was when we heard that the Berlin Wall was being torn down live on television, 1 of the most significant news events of that year. Then back into the closet it went.

I can't tell you the joy that Lana and I had that first year, just the two of us in our 1-bedroom apartment in Houston, Texas. It freed us up to spend all kinds of time together, whether it was cooking dinner, playing games, cleaning dishes, going out or making love. Someone had given us money to buy a new TV as a wedding present, which we saved to get one when our first year was over. But we enjoyed our life without a TV so much that we kept it that way for several years until we finally decided to buy one so we could watch movies or teach the kids. After 23 years, we still watched very little TV, nor did our kids, because we just never developed the a habit. (And when we did start watching TV again, we were shocked at how much more negative the content on TV seemed to have turned in just those few short years.)

Let me add here again that these are suggestions that you'll have to adapt to your own situation, whether it's limiting time on the Internet or social media, or watching only a set number of shows or sporting events per month, or whatever it takes to give you the best shot at increasing your time to communicate. As the Apostle Paul reminded the Corinthians:

> *"Everything is permissible"—but not everything is beneficial. "Everything is permissible"—but not everything is constructive (1 Corinthians 10:23).*

3) Combine your bank accounts. Communication is the #1 cause for divorce, but finances are a close second. Lana and I were encouraged at the beginning of our marriage to combine our bank accounts and share a checkbook. This meant that we had to talk about our purchases with each other so there were no surprises. This also kept us in check from making whimsical or unnecessary purchases. By combining our bank accounts we were also able to better save our money and make a priority of helping to fulfill each other's dreams, whether it was a special trip for an anniversary or a missions trip to another country or a new vehicle when we needed one.

Because we had to make our decisions together, we simply made wiser decisions. Although it was harder at first because we had to work together, it kept us from having the mentality that "this is my money" and "this is your money." We realized early on that "this is God's money" and we wanted to spend it in the best way possible. As King David said to God:

"Everything comes from You, and we have given You only what comes from Your hand" (1 Chronicles 29:14b).

This may not apply to every situation or every stage of life, but it's important to do something to make sure your finances enhance your marriage and not take away from it. For instance, I noticed that Lana was supportive whenever I was asked to speak anywhere special, but that doing so cost her in terms of my time and energy. So I began giving her any money I received from these extra speaking engagements, rather than using it for our every day bills. It was a simple way to make sure the money we received was working for our marriage, not against it.

4) Never use the "D" word: Divorce. There's a funny line in the movie, *It's a Wonderful Life,* when the house maid Annie gives some money to George Bailey when he's in dire straights. Annie says, "I've been saving this money for a divorce, if ever I got a husband!" It's a funny line for a movie, but it's a terrible line for real life. Sometimes you might be tempted to hold things back from your spouse "just in case things don't work out." But those very things that you're holding back might be the pathway to greater intimacy if they were shared, whether it's money or secrets or simply giving yourself as fully as possible to your spouse.

If you're committed to marriage for life, which God certainly is, never use the word "divorce," especially as a threat. Some people hold onto that option and use it as a weapon in an argument. But it's not a weapon. Jesus said that Moses allowed for divorce only because of the hardness of people's hearts, but that it wasn't always that way from the beginning (see Matthew 19:8).

If you're struggling in your marriage, keep your hearts soft and tender by looking for other ways to deal with your problems, whether you look to God, the Bible, prayer, counselors, friends or perhaps even time away. But not divorce. God says in the Bible:

"I hate divorce" (Malachi 2:16).

And anyone who's been through one knows why. When I've counseled couples for marriage, I've sometimes told them that I'm glad to bless their marriage, but on one condition: that if they ever consider a divorce, that they have to come back to me first and get my blessing for that, too. Then I let them know that in all my years of counseling people, I've never felt led to bless a divorce, even in some of the most intense situations. I've always felt that God can work through even the most intense situations, especially if both people are willing to do so.

5) Confess your sins quickly. I heard about a man who walked across America. He said his toughest moments weren't when he was walking through the rain or snow or to the top of a tall mountain. He said his toughest times were when he got tiny grains of sand in his shoes. Unless he stopped to regularly dump out the sand, those tiny grains would rub against his feet until blisters formed and then he would suffer for days or weeks in extreme pain until his feet healed.

I heard this story in a sermon about marriage one Sunday morning, in the context of confessing even those small sins in our lives to our spouse, dumping them out of our shoes before they rubbed enough to cause more severe pain. I immediately thought of a particular friendship I had with someone that I enjoyed, perhaps a little too much. There was nothing sinful going on, but the fact that this friendship came to mind as I heard this story made me wonder if maybe I should confess it to Lana and ask her what to do about it. I didn't want to mention it though, because I was afraid the best solution would be to step back from this friendship all together, and I didn't want to lose the friendship.

But after a few days of praying, I realized that even though this issue seemed like no big deal, as small as a grain of sand, I knew I'd rather dump it out now than let it possibly endanger my marriage down the road. I confessed it to Lana and we agreed it would be best for me to back off from the friendship. Even though it was a good friendship in my life, I felt so much freer after stepped back and it never caused another problem again. Confess any sins right away, even if they're as small as a grain of sand. As the Bible says,

"Therefore confess your sins to each other and pray for each other so that you may be healed" (James 5:16).

6) Love your way through any "irreconcilable differences." I once heard about an interviewer who asked several couples who had gotten a divorce how many "irreconcilable differences" they had in their marriage; things that they were simply never able to agree upon. The average answer was 5 or 6 "irreconcilable differences." The interviewer then asked the same question of several couples who were still together after 40, 50 and 60 years. Their answer? 5 or 6! It wasn't the number of irreconcilable differences that made the difference in whether the couples stayed together or not, but their commitment to love each other through them.

We're all unique. We all have different backgrounds and life experiences. It's no surprise that we think differently on various topics as well. It's part of life and it's all part of what makes being married work so much better than being alone for so many people, because they can each bring their best ideas to table. But invariably this means that many other ideas have to be left on the table, even good ones. Lana and I agreed on a lot of things, but there were probably 5 or 6 that we still never agreed on in all our years together.

We're all like porcupines, with our various differences and sins poking out of us all the time. And when we get close enough to each other, there's a good chance we'll get poked. Yet even porcupines find a way to have baby porcupines. How do they do it? Very carefully!

Don't let your sins and differences cause you to lose your commitment to a lifetime of marriage no matter what. Love your way through them instead. As the Bible says:

"Above all, love each other deeply, because love covers over a multitude of sins" (John 15:13).

7) Invite and allow Jesus to love your spouse through you. When I married Lana, I knew without a doubt that she was a gift from God to me. But I also realized that if she was a gift from God to me, then perhaps I was a gift from God to her, too. As such, I often wondered what Jesus would want me to do for her if He were here on earth, for the Bible says that we are the body of Christ and

He wants to be able to live His life through us to touch others (see 1 Corinthians 12).

So when Lana would lay in bed at night, exhausted from a long day of taking care of everyone else around her, I would think, "What Would Jesus Do?" If Jesus was here, what would He want to say to her? What would He want to do for her? How would He minister to the deepest needs of her heart right now? Then I would try to let Jesus use me to love her, using my words to speak to her, my hands to stroke her head, my ears to listen to what she'd been going through during the day.

WWJD (What Would Jesus Do) might seem like a trite acronym to put on a bracelet or a bumper sticker, but it's only trite if we make it so. If we take it seriously—and realize it's exactly what God *wants* us to ask at all times and in all situations, especially with our spouse—it can change the dynamics of every relationship that we have.

As I was writing this message to you today, I happened to hear from the wife of a couple I had married several years ago. She shared with me that that this was the single most important tip she learned back then, and that it was the #1 thing that was getting her through the mess she and her husband were in right now, inviting and allowing Jesus to love her spouse through her.

Just as God has placed your spouse in your life as a gift to you, He has placed you in your spouse's life as a gift to them. Invite and allow Jesus to love your spouse through you. As the Bible says:

"Now you are the body of Christ, and each one of you is a part of it" (1 Corinthians 12:27).

That's enough tips for now (it's enough for a lifetime, really!) But in the next several chapters I'll share some more tips that can be just as significant as these. Then I'll wrap it all up in Chapter 6 with those 3 simple words that serve as the glue to hold all the other tips together.

Chapter 2

In this chapter I'm sharing just 4 tips with you. I've grouped these together because each one is related to how you balance your needs and callings with the needs and callings of your spouse. These can help to ensure that your marriage is a true partnership to help you *both* accomplish all that God has put on your hearts to do.

With that in mind, here are tips #8 through 11 for how to have a stronger marriage.

8) Be willing to live for your spouse. I spoke to a man who was divorcing his wife. She wanted to move to another state to fulfill some of her dreams, but he didn't want to. They were at a stalemate and this was the last straw.

I asked him, "If someone threatened to kill your wife, would you be willing to die for her?"

"Yes, of course," he replied.

Then I asked, "If you would be willing to die for her, would you be willing to live for her?"

We talked again shortly thereafter and he put his faith in Christ. He reconciled with his wife and they moved across the country. As Jesus told His disciples:

"Greater love has no one than this, that he lay down his life for his friends" (John 15:13).

Then Jesus proved His love for His friends by laying down His life for them.

Surprisingly, "laying down your life" doesn't always mean giving up your own dreams and plans, too. For Jesus also said,

"For whoever wants to save his life will lose it, but whoever loses his life for Me will find it" (Matthew 16:25).

Sometimes it's by helping your spouse achieve their dreams that you'll be better able to fulfill your own dreams. If God is the one who has put special dreams and desires within both you and your spouse, then He'll find a way to accomplish those dreams and desires for both of you, too.

9) Help your spouse achieve their goals. This may sound like the previous tip, but the difference is that sometimes you'll have to take the initiative to help your spouse achieve their goals. It may be that God has put you in their life just for this purpose, because He knew they would need your unique help. After God created Adam, He said:

"It's not good for the Man to be alone; I'll make him a helper, a companion" (Genesis 2:18, MSG).

One of the main purposes for marriage, according to God, is so we won't have to do life alone; that we'll have a helper and a companion along the way.

Lana was both of those things to me: a wonderful companion and a terrific helper. She helped me do things I could never have done on my own, whether it was building a family or launching a ministry or giving me regular feedback and encouragement on my writing and speaking and planning and dreaming. At the same time, I was able to help her achieve some of her goals. Over the years, however, I realized that she still had other dreams and desires for her life which would never be realized if I didn't step in to give her a boost. She wanted to do missions work in Africa, visit the Holy Land and make a movie about the life of St. Nicholas.

But with all of her other responsibilities, those dreams seemed either distant or impossible. So I sat down with her and began to pray about each one, asking God how I could help her achieve her dreams. Within a few years, I was able to help her take a missions trip to Africa, visit the Holy Land twice and write out the story of the life of St. Nicholas, which we planned to use as the basis for a movie someday. When we found out that Lana had cancer, I can't tell you how thankful I was that I had stepped in to help her fulfill those dreams while she was still able to do them—and I'd encourage you to do the same.

10) Remember your marriage is a calling, too. I think a word of caution is in order here, too. Be careful when considering giving up one type of "calling" to follow another. I shared my story with a group one day about quitting my job and going into full-time ministry. A woman came up to me afterwards to tell me how excited she was because God was calling her to do the same thing. After congratulating her for being willing to take this step of faith, I asked her what kept her from doing it before. She said, "Well, my husband won't like it because I'm going to have to move and leave him behind."

"As in divorce?" I asked.

"Yes," she said, and she looked at the floor.

I said, "Don't forsake one type of calling (your marriage) to fulfill another. If this is from God, He'll help you to do both."

Your marriage is a calling just as much as any other kind of "calling." When I quit my job and went into full-time ministry, I knew for me that meant living on faith for all of our financial provision (we all live on faith, actually; it's just that sometimes we're more acutely aware of it than others). But I also knew I was called to my marriage with Lana.

So I wrote Lana a letter, telling her that even though I felt called by God to do this ministry, I also felt called by God to marry her and to take care of her as best I could. I committed to her, right at the beginning of our ministry, that if ever she felt she wasn't being cared for because of the ministry that I was doing, then I would quit doing ministry or I would find another way to do it so that I could care for her better.

I didn't want to shortchange one calling to fulfill another. As the Bible says rather forcefully:

"Anyone who does not provide for their relatives, and especially for their own household, has denied the faith and is worse than an unbeliever" (1 *Timothy 5:8*).

Lana never had to exercise her right to pull out the letter and pull me out of ministry, although she came close a few times. And whenever she did, we prayed together and I filled out applications for other jobs. God always made a way for me to fulfill both callings, however, so I could keep loving her well and keep doing ministry well. I knew that if I had to neglect one calling to fulfill another, then I was probably doing something wrong, and if God had called me to both, He would help me to find a way to do both.

11) Remember that God is the provider for both of you. If you haven't noticed, each of these tips builds on the others. While there's a lot that you can do for your spouse, you can't do everything! There are some things only God can do. Ultimately, He's the one who provides for you both. As the Bible says,

"The earth is the LORD's, and everything in it…" (Psalm 24:1a).

When I was first dating Lana, we relied on each other for everything: our conversation, our intimacy, our affirmation, our affection. But when God broke us up for a period of time, we learned to rely on Him as the ultimate source of everything in our lives, including each other. When we finally came back together and eventually got married, we had a new awareness that God was the source of all we needed, even if He used one or the other of us to meet that need. He was still the source of it all.

I was reminded of how much God loved Lana one morning after we had had a funny conversation the day before. Her car had broken down and we needed to find another, but there was no way we could afford one. She told me the kind of car she really wanted to get. She had never cared about makes or models of cars before, just whatever would get her from Point A to Point B. When I looked at the prices of used models online, I thought, "Good luck with that!"

A friend of ours told us when he sent his daughter off to college, the only thing he had to give her were his prayers and these words: "The same God who takes care of me will take care of you." God did His part, My friend did what he could do, his daughter did what she could do, and God did what only He could do. 4 years later she had a college degree!

So that night as I prayed for Lana and the car she wanted, I said at the end, rather jokingly, "Well, you've got my prayers! The same God who takes care of me will take care of you!" Then I rolled over and fell asleep.

The joke was on me, though, when the very next morning I pulled into the parking lot for a men's group at church and a man pulled in right after me—driving the exact car that Lana had told me she wanted. He had never visited the group before and I had never seen another car like this around town. It was the same exact make, model and color that Lana had wanted!

I told the man that my wife was talking about getting a car just like that and he said he was actually thinking of selling it! I had to shake my head and confess to God that I had forgotten how much *He* loved her, too—even more than I did—and that *He* was the one who provided everything for her, just like He provided everything for me. Although we didn't buy that man's car, God made a way for us to buy another one—the same model, make and color—within just a few months of those feeble prayers. God really does love our spouse even more than we love them, and He loves to surprise and delight them, just as He loves to surprise and delight us.

Sometimes we make the mistake of trying too hard to please our spouse, only to fall short again and again, when what we really need to do is to trust God that He will provide for them, even when we can't. So do your best and trust God with the rest.

That's it for today, and probably more than

enough "home work" for you to think about for this chapter! In the next chapter, I'll share only 1 tip so you can focus on it exclusively.

CHAPTER 3

One of the questions I'm asked most about marriage is "How did you know that Lana was 'the one' for you?" Today I'll share that answer with you in Tip #12 for how to have a stronger marriage.

But don't think that today's tip is only for those who are considering marriage. Even if you've been married a long, long time, today's tip can help to re-energize your marriage as you remember why you chose your spouse in the first place.

With that in mind, here's tip #12 for how to have a stronger marriage.

12) Choose well (and remember why you chose the one you did). Next to your decision to follow Christ, choosing who to marry is the 2nd most important decision you'll ever make in your life. It's a decision that will affect you for the rest of your life, and it's a decision that will affect generations of people long after you're gone.

I read a book before I got married that scared me, and for good reason: I wasn't ready to get married. Even though I loved Lana deeply, this book helped me see the enormity of the decision to get married and how it would affect my life from that moment on. The book was called *The Mystery of Marriage* by Mike Mason. Mike said:

> *"A marriage, or a marriage partner, may be compared to a great tree growing right up through the center of one's living room. It is something that is just there, and it is huge, and everything has been built around it, and wherever one happens to be going—to the fridge, to bed, to the bathroom, or out the front door—the tree has to be taken into account. It cannot be gone through; it must respectfully be gone around. It is somehow bigger and stronger than oneself. True, it could be chopped down, but not without tearing the house apart. And certainly it is beautiful, unique, exotic: but also, let's face it, it is at times an enormous inconvenience.*
>
> *So there are many things that can be said about*

one's life's mate, but finally, irrevocably, the one definite thing that needs to be said is that he or she is always there. And that, while it may be common enough in the world of trees, is among us human beings a rather remarkable state of affairs" (Mike Mason, *The Mystery of Marriage*, p. 39).

The book goes on to describe how nothing in life does more to expose our pride, failings and weaknesses than being married. Our selfishness is exposed at every turn. As the Bible says:

"As iron sharpens iron, so one person sharpens another" (Proverbs 27:17).

As helpful as it is for us to be sharpened, the process of chipping away at the ugly and unsightly things in our lives can be painful. I just wasn't ready. I remember going to my brother and sister-in-law's wedding, watching them take their vows for a lifetime and thinking, "I can't do this! I just can't do it!" It wasn't that I didn't love Lana, but that I couldn't imagine giving up the idea of just living my life for myself.

In the months that followed, however, God

began to show me all that I would gain by being married. I had recently put my faith in Christ, and I was already seeing the fruit of having invited Him into my life and taking His thoughts into account before acting on my own. I was eventually convinced that marriage could be worth giving up whatever independence I had before. The question then became, "Who does God want me to marry?"

Although the Bible gives us certain baseline criteria for choosing a spouse, such as believers marrying other believers (2 Corinthians 6:14a and 1 Kings 11:2b), not marrying close relatives (Leviticus 18:6-19), and marrying someone who can help God fulfill His recreative design for the world (Leviticus 18:22-23 and Romans 1:26-27), it doesn't tell us which person, specifically, who God wants us to marry. At least I didn't think so. For that, I knew I would have to rely on God's Holy Spirit. And I've found that He is more than happy to help us—as long as we're willing to listen.

So how did I know that Lana was "the one"? For me, my answer came after months of asking God to speak to me clearly if she was the one that He wanted me to marry. I had already come to the conclusion that I wanted to marry her, but I needed to know for sure what God wanted, because I knew that He knew both of us better than we knew ourselves.

One morning I sat down in my bedroom to read my Bible, but didn't know what to read. I had just finished reading my Bible from cover to cover a few days earlier for the first time in my life, and I wasn't sure where to start reading again. So I decided to start over at the beginning.

Lana had come to visit me that morning, as we had already been out to watch a friend run a race in downtown Houston. We decided to take some time to pray on our own before going on with the day, so she sat on the couch in the living room with her Bible, and I went to the bedroom with mine. This was a refreshingly new practice for both of us in that previous year.

I opened up my Bible to the first page and began to read again about how God created the world, and how God created Adam, the first man on earth. God put Adam in a beautiful garden and asked him to take care of it. But God saw that even in the midst of this beautiful setting, surrounded by all kinds of spectacular things, Adam was still alone:

"The LORD God said, 'It is not good for the man to be alone. I will make a helper suitable for him'" (Genesis 2:18).

So God created Eve and brought her to Adam.

Even though I had heard this story since I was a kid, this was the first time I had seen it from God's perspective. As I read about Adam being alone in the garden, my heart fell as God's must have fallen, when He saw how lonely Adam was. Then my heart rose again, as God's must have risen, when God created Eve and brought her to Adam. I imagined the smile on Adam's face must have about a mile wide!

As I pictured this scene in my mind, I suddenly had an intense awareness that God was looking down at me just as He had looked at Adam. There I was, surrounded by all kinds of spectacular things, but I was still alone. In that moment, God spoke to my heart. The words seemed to leap off the page, and I felt that God had done the same for me: He had created a woman just for me and He had brought her directly to me. She was sitting in the very next room! After months of praying, I knew that I knew that God really did want to fulfill the desires of my heart and He really did want me to marry Lana.

I got up off the floor and ran down the hall. I didn't stop to look in the mirror as I ran, but I'm sure if I did, the smile on my face would have been about a mile wide. I told Lana what God had told me through the story of Adam and Eve. We talked and we cried and I asked her to marry me right on the spot. To my delight, she said "Yes!" and we spent the rest of that incredible day together walking and talking and riding paddle boats in the rain at Miller Park.

My eyes still water as I think about it again 25 years later. Even though I didn't have a ring to give her, and we didn't have a candle-light dinner, I had something that was even more precious to me: I had a word from God that Lana was "the one." I can't tell you how many times I've come back to that story over the years, both in good times and in hard times, and how it has re-energized my love for and commitment to Lana.

For Lana, the story was much simpler: she said she knew from the day she met me that God wanted her to marry me. She said that as soon as we met, there on the 2nd floor of David Kinley Hall at the University of Illinois, that these words immediately popped into her mind: "That's the man you're going to marry."

She said it was the wording that made her realize it was from God, and the way that the words came into her mind. She said the words seemed to come into her mind out of the blue, and they were spoken in the 3rd person: "That's the man you're going to marry." She said that if it was her own thought, she would have said to herself, "That's the man I'm going to marry!" But she didn't, and the words were clear: "That's the man you're going to marry." She was so convinced that she went home that night and called one of her best friends to tell her she had just met the man she was going to marry. And she was right!

I tell you these stories not because I think God will speak to you in the exact same way, but to give you confidence that God can speak to you, if you're willing to listen to Him. God's Holy Spirit really is alive and active. And, believe it or not, God wants you to know who to marry even more than you want to know it. He has a bigger stake in the outcome of your life than you do, and He knows you and every other person on the planet even better than you know yourself.

I had been diligently seeking God for months for His answer (after dating Lana for years before finally coming to the place of asking God what He wanted for our relationship). And Lana had been praying ever since she was a child for a man to marry who would be like Jesus to her, not that I was ever close to that, but in her eyes at least, she felt that I was the answer to all those prayers.

Once I knew that Lana was the one for me, I knew there was never any going back. I was committed to planting that tree of marriage right in the center of my living room, and I was happier about it than I can possibly tell you. I never used the D word (Divorce) because I knew that wasn't an option. I knew that for better or worse, neither of us were going away, and we were going to have to work through anything that came our way together. And I couldn't have been happier about it.

Just like the words "God will never leave you alone" can be either a blessing or a curse depending on how you look at it, the idea of being with another person 24/7 for the rest of your life can be a blessing or a curse, too, depending on how you look at it. That's why it's so important to remember why you chose the one you did in the first place, because it can help restore the way you look at your marriage, not as a curse of always having someone else around, but as a blessing of always having someone else around.

If you're still considering who to marry, I want to encourage you to choose well. No decision, other than your decision to follow Christ, is as important. And no decision this important is one that God wants you to take lightly. He would love to help you know who to marry, for He has a vested interest in the outcome of both of your lives.

For those of you who have already made your choice of who to marry and who are now living out that choice, perhaps even wondering if you made the right choice or not, I'd like to encourage you to look back and remember why you made that choice in the first place.

What was it that drew you to your spouse? What made him or her so special to you when you first met or when you first started dating? What did God speak to you about him or her along the way? What feelings or emotions stirred within you that made you want to make this commitment to be together forever? Choosing well is important, but re-membering can be just as important to help-ing you stay committed to your choice. As Nehemiah said about the Israelites who went back on some of their earlier choices:

"They refused to listen and failed to remember the miracles You performed among them" (Nehemiah 9:17).

They didn't listen to God, and they failed to remember the miracles He performed among them. Don't be like that! Listen to God, and then remember what God has told you.

I'm not saying it's easy to choose who to marry or to stay married after you've made that choice, and I'm not saying that people won't surprise you down the road with actions and decisions that catch us totally off guard.

In fact, I'm saying just the opposite. I'm saying that none of us really know what we're getting into when we commit to living with another person for the rest of our lives. None of us really know what's in the hearts of other people living on the planet, let alone what's in our own hearts. But God knows.

God knows what's in our hearts, and He knows how to guide and direct us if we're willing to listen. God also knows how to redeem ANY situation and ANY decision we ever make, even the bad ones. In fact, that's why He sent Jesus to die: to redeem us from the poor choices we make, the sins we've committed along the way, so that we can live a new and abundant life, both here on earth and in heaven forever. No matter how you've arrived at the place you're in right now, you can trust Him to redeem and restore it and to help make it right.

But if you're not married yet, do yourself and everyone else around you a huge favor: Choose well! Listen to God, then remember the miracles He's done among you.

Chapter 4

I was going to call this tip "How to have a fair fight," which captures the essence of the message well. But the idea behind this tip isn't to help you fight better; the idea is to help you express your feelings better so you and your spouse can truly hear what each other is saying and do something about it before it becomes a fight.

I think you'll find this tip applies to any of your relationships, not just your marriage. In fact, I heard from a single woman who wrote to tell me as I was writing this series to say how surprised she was that God was speaking to her through these marriage tips, even though she's not married. She wrote:

"I was hesitant at first to read this devotional as I'm not married. I was just scrolling through and saw a part about Lana and yourself getting a car and about marriage being a calling. So I decided to

start from the top for I believed God wanted me to learn a thing or two and also to be encouraged as I was feeling a bit down and questioning my future. I enjoyed it and it made me laugh how God worked out your differences, even your breaking up and eventually getting married. That gave me hope since I'm single and struggling relationship wise. My concern about my future especially is that I really want to change my car and I laughed with tears coming to my eyes when you said about Lana's desires for a car and how you reassured her about God working and providing for you and He will do the same for her. I like the part too about your partner understanding your purpose & dreams and how God can use you to help each other reach their potential and how God can use each other to bring about change & transformation. I have always believed that. Thanks for sharing your testimony. I must read the 7 points from earlier and see what else God wants me to know. God bless!"

So whether you apply this tip to your marriage or to any relationship, I hope you'll read today's tip closely and let God speak to your heart.

13) Watch your timing, tone and words. Lana and I didn't fight often, and when we did, we tried to do so in private. This may have given others the impression that we never fought, but that's not true. I will say, though, that we were able to avoid many of the all-out fights that others experience simply by following some advice that we learned during pre-marital counseling and some other wisdom that we learned for ourselves from the Bible.

This tip involves 3 aspects of how you express your feelings to each other: your timing, your tone and your words.

First, watch your timing. It's important, of course, to share your feelings and not to stuff them down inside. We all have feelings and we want others to respect our feelings. But it's also important to consider the timing of when to share those feelings. Even Jesus didn't say everything that was on His heart to His disciples, but took into account when they would best receive what He had to say. Jesus said:

"I have much more to say to you, more than you can now bear" (John 16:12).

Jesus eventually did share everything on His heart, and He told the disciples that He would send His Holy Spirit later to remind them of everything He said. But He did so at a time when He knew they could best receive it.

Lana and I found that if we had something important to share with each other, especially if it was potentially explosive, that it was best to talk about it when we were both fresh and alert and able to talk about it rationally. We seemed to have our worst conversations when one or both of us were tired and worn out or when we had pressing deadlines that had to be met. It was better if we could realize the timing was bad and set a time to talk later when we could truly listen to each other.

Second, it's important to watch your tone. It's easy to jump to conclusions and blame your spouse for things they didn't even know were wrong. In America, we love the idea of being "innocent until proven guilty." But in marriage, we often jump to the conclusion that our spouse is guilty and we start an argument based on that assumed guilt rather than simply explaining what we're feeling. The

Bible talks about the importance of tone when it says:

"A gentle answer turns away wrath, but a harsh word stirs up anger" (Proverbs 15:1).

When I came to Lana with gentleness, simply sharing something that I was feeling, I was usually met with a gentle response in return. But when I came to her with a harsh or accusatory tone, it stirred up a harsh or angry response. This is a simple law of nature and it's a simple law of communication: "For every action there is an equal and opposite reaction."

Instead of looking straight at your spouse and assuming they are the problem, it's better to turn shoulder to shoulder and address the problem together. It might even help to remind yourself and your spouse, "I know you're not my enemy. I'm fighting for you, not against you." By simply reminding yourselves of this truth, you can often diffuse the bomb that might otherwise explode.

I remember being called to a friend's house late one night. She and her husband were in the middle of an argument—and it was bad.

In fact, when I walked in, I wondered if she should have called the police instead of me.

But as I sat down with both of them and listened to what they were arguing about, it turned out that the husband was trying to tell his wife that he wished he could spend more time with her, because she was often out helping other people in need. They were talking past each other, though, because they were talking about 2 different things. The truth was that they both wanted to do something good; they just needed to work on how to achieve those good things together.

Here the wife thought her husband hated her for wanting to help others, when the truth was that he loved her so much he wanted to spend more time with her! And he loved that she wanted to help other people, but he just wished she would spend more of that energy on him, rather than depleting it all before she got home. By talking through both of their desires, without accusation or harsh words, they were able to find a way to move forward and help meet each of their desires more fully.

This story leads to the third aspect of how to have a fair fight, which is to watch the words you choose. Here's a simple phrase you can memorize and, if you start using it today, you'll find your conversations will go much smoother immediately. The phrase is:

"I feel ... when ... because ... "

This focuses the issue on you and your thoughts and feelings rather than on the other person.

In the story I shared above about the couple fighting, the husband started with an accusatory tone by saying "You're always out helping other people!" To which his wife immediately reacted by saying, "What's wrong with helping other people?!?" Then she started listing all the good and godly reasons to help others. She was also stung by the word "always" and said, "I'm not *always* out helping other people!!!" because she began to recall how many the times she stayed home to help him or their family. (It's better just to drop the words "you always" or "you never" from arguments, because the other person can usually think of at least a few times when they did or did not do whatever they're being accused of doing).

But because of the husband's wording (and

probably his timing and tone, based on the lateness and intensity of the conversation), he had inadvertently derailed the conversation from the beginning and they began squabbling over side issues. Rather than starting the sentence with the accusatory words "You always...," consider if he had started by saying, "I feel...," and then filled in the blanks that followed:

"I feel hurt when you go out to help others because I'd like to spend more time with you myself."

That's really what the husband was trying to say, but it came out as anger and jealousy rather than love and affection. By blaming her for wanting to help others, he put her on the defensive from the start, rather than simply expressing what he really wanted, which was to spend more time with her.

Using the words "I feel … when … because…" changes the tenor of your conversations immediately and helps you get closer to meeting your own needs sooner than if you get sidetracked on secondary conversations. You may still need to have those secondary conversations, but you'll realize that they are just that: secondary. The main thing is to be able to express what you're feeling, without blame or accusation, by describing how you feel when the other person does or does not do certain things.

Your choice of words can make all the difference, not only for yourself, but also for the other person. The Bible says:

"A word fitly spoken is like apples of gold in settings of silver" (Proverbs 25:11, NKJV).

Which means that words that are well timed and placed are beautiful to behold.

As an exercise to help you think through your words the next time you need to express something you're feeling, imagine a conversation that you may be currently having with your spouse (or co-worker or friend), whether it's a conversation you've been having out loud or if it's still just in your head, and try to rephrase what you're feeling using the words "I feel... when... because."

Think hard about what you're really feeling and why. Rather than accusing the other person in your head, imagine that you're truly just trying to express your feelings and what triggers those feelings.

I feel lonely
I feel frustrated
I feel hurt
I feel unappreciated

when you come home late
when you move my piles
when you forget to do what I ask
when you correct me

because I want to go to bed with you
because I don't know where things are when I need them
because I want to know that you care about me
because I'm trying hard to do the right thing

You can see how each of these statements could lead to further discussion and exploration of why the person feels what they feel and finding a solution that is beneficial for both people.

You might be thinking, "That sounds like a lot of work," and you'd be right! It is! But the payoff is worth it.

In woodworking there's a saying, "Measure twice; cut once." When you carefully take the time to measure a piece of wood twice and then cut it only once, you save yourself a whole lot of time patching things up later. The same could be said of your words: "Think twice; speak once." As the Bible says:

"Everyone should be quick to listen, slow to speak and slow to become angry" (James 1:19b).

Although it takes extra time and effort to think through your timing, your tone and your words, you'll save yourself a whole lot of time and effort in patching things up later!

Coming up next, tips #14 and 15!

Chapter 5

Today I'm sharing the last 2 tips of these 15 tips for a stronger marriage. Then in next chapter I'll conclude with 3 words that tie all the other tips together.

But before I get started on today's tips, I want to let you know that Tip #15 is perhaps the most significant tip I ever received before getting married. It's also one of the most delicate to talk about because it has to do with physical intimacy.

For the sake of modesty, and for the sake of getting this message through any spam filters when I first sent this message out by email, I've simply used the phrase "physical intimacy" to describe the physical union between a husband and wife, and I've used the term "self pleasure" to describe the act of touching yourself in a way that brings you physical pleasure when you are alone. (Now you can see why this tip is so delicate! But I assure you, what you're going to read today could significantly alter the way you interact with your spouse from this day forward!)

With that preface in mind, here are Tips #14 and 15.

14) Commit to doing something to delight your spouse on a regular basis. Before I married Lana, I promised to give her a back rub every night, which was something that she absolutely loved. It worked out well for both of us, because she loved being touched, and I loved touching her! For 23 years I kept that commitment and it was one of the best things I ever promised to do, both for her and for myself.

Those back rubs also led to other kinds of intimacy, setting the tone for our bedtime conversations and often culminating in physical passion. By blessing Lana in this one way, I received all kinds of blessings back.

I also committed to making breakfast for her every morning, something which she loved at the time we got married, too. But as time and the seasons of life changed, she began to prefer other things instead, like sleeping in a little longer while I made breakfast for the kids after she had spent the night nursing a baby! I say this to say that some of our commitments may change over time, but the point is to intentionally commit to doing *something* to delight your spouse on a regular basis. It smooths out the ebbs and flows of life and ensures there's joy in the midst of anything else that might be going on.

For her part, Lana had made a commitment before we got married, too, but one that she didn't tell me about until many years into our marriage. She just did it. She committed to herself that she would go to bed every night at the same time that I went to bed. She had watched other couples live their lives in separate bedrooms for years and she saw the devastating effects that this had on their relationships. So she told herself she was going to do whatever she could to try to ensure that didn't happen in her marriage.

Of course, this ensured she got her nightly back rub! But even more, it meant that we had time to talk and pray together every night; it meant that we were available for physical intimacy on a regular basis; and it increased the likelihood of having a big family like she always wanted!

You and your spouse may have a different set of things you could do to delight one other. If you're not sure what would delight them, just ask them! Then make a commitment to doing something to delight them in the way they'd love to be delighted on a regular basis. As the Bible says:

"...love one another deeply, from the heart" (1 Peter 1:22b).

15) Make physical intimacy with your spouse the best that it can be. After I was engaged to Lana, I set up an appointment to meet with a man who had counseled many, many people through marital issues regarding their physical intimacy. I met with him specifically because I wanted to ensure that I did everything possible to safeguard our physical relationship and to make it the best that it could possibly be.

One of the most important tips he shared with me was to consider making a commitment to myself and to Lana that I would not engage in self pleasure, but that I would only experience physical pleasure when I was with her. Many men, he said, go into marriage thinking that they'll be able to be intimate with their wife any time they want. But the reality is that it just doesn't work that way! And because of that, many spouses decide to simply please themselves whenever they want.

This man told me that he had met with numerous groups of women to discuss issues like this, and asked them what they would think if they knew their husbands were pleasing themselves when they weren't together. Nearly every woman in every group said they would feel hurt by this, or they would wonder what they were doing wrong that their husbands would do this, or they would wonder *what else* their husbands might be doing physically when they weren't together.

Then this man went on to tell me about the blessings couples experienced who had committed to enjoying physical pleasure only when they were together. He said it wasn't necessary that they engage in full physical intimacy every time, but that they were at least to be with each other and enjoy the closeness of their bodies. Couples who made this commitment built up trust, lowered barriers to in-

timacy and brought about a lifetime of fulfill-
ment for each other, both inside and outside
of the bedroom.

Since I had never even considered how this
might play out in marriage, I didn't know what
to think. But this man had thrown down a
gauntlet, a challenge, and I had to decide
whether or not I was going to pick it up.
After talking some more about this with another friend and then with Lana, I decided it
was worth a try. So before Lana and I were
married, I committed to her that I would not
engage in self pleasure, but reserve all physical
pleasure only for when I was with her. If for
any reason I fell down in this commitment, I
committed to confessing it to her before the
day was out.

I can attest to the fact that this one tip
alone helped me perhaps more than any of
the others. Why? Because each of these tips
are interrelated and physical intimacy is at the
core of what makes marriage unique among
all other relationships. So when there's a
breakdown in one area of your relationship, it
often affects your physical intimacy as well.
In order to ensure I would be able to enjoy
the physical pleasures of marriage, I knew I

would have to nurture the other areas of my marriage, too. As the saying goes:

"The grass ain't always greener on the other side; it's greener where you water it."

Here's how some of the tips I've mentioned already helped to water our physical intimacy. For instance, by putting our TV in the closet for our first year, it freed up all kinds of time to have meaningful conversations and enjoy soothing back rubs, which often led to physical intimacy. By going to bed every night at the same time as each other and by praying together before we fell asleep, we were able to draw closer spiritually and that drew us closer physically. By confessing our sins quickly to each other, we built up trust between us and kept guilt and shame at bay. By inviting Jesus to use our hands and eyes and words as if they were His very own, we were able to keep our touches and kisses as tender and life-giving as possible.

This isn't to say that it was easy for me to keep this challenge. Even though my physical intimacy with Lana was incredible from day 1, there were still a few times in our first year of marriage when I fell back into old habits of pleasing myself when I was alone or away from home. It seemed like a quick and easy way to release some of the tension in other areas of my life.

Yet I still wanted to give this idea an honest try, and because of my promise to Lana, I followed through with the rest of it and confessed it to Lana each time before the day was out. The first time I had to confess it to her it was more difficult and embarrassing than I imagined. The second time was even more difficult. So after just a few confessions like this, I was able to break the habit and keep my commitment for the rest of our 23 years of marriage.

I'm not telling you this out of some kind of prudish purity, but simply to let you know that it's possible! And believe me, my passions and temptations are just as strong as any other man's! But until my conversation with this marriage counselor, I had never even thought about the idea.

I also tell you this because I can't describe the multitude of ways this one commitment helped our marriage. Here are just a few:

1) This gave us both confidence that I had control over my body, rather than my body having control over me. This helped Lana to trust me to not cross the line of having physical pleasure with someone else, because I wouldn't even cross it with myself.

2) This kept me from turning on the TV in a hotel room when I was away from home, or from buying a magazine that I shouldn't have bought, or from downloading a video that I shouldn't have downloaded. Even though these things certainly crossed my mind and were ever-present opportunit-ies, there was never any point to engaging in these activities since I knew that they would never cul-minate in physical pleasure.

3) This ensured that the physical side of our mar-ital relationship was fully alive and vibrant throughout our entire marriage. Roger Staubach, the famous quarterback, was once asked how he felt when one of his teammates always seemed to have a different woman on his arm every night. Roger said, "I'm sure I'm just as sexually active as he is. The difference is that all of mine is with one woman." Touchdown, Roger! The joy of my physical intimacy with Lana, and the trust that we

*built into our relationship because of this one com-
mitment, was worth anything it might have cost me
in terms of giving up fleeting pleasures on my own.*

While I can't say if this commitment is
something that you should make, or that it
will have the same impact on your marriage, I
do want to encourage you to do whatever you
can to nurture the physical intimacy of your
marriage.

By the way, one of the best books we read
before getting married that helped us in our
sexual relationship throughout our entire marriage was called *Intended For Pleasure* by Ed and
Gaye Wheat. The book contains many helpful tips for making your sex life the best that it
can be. I highly recommend it for any married couple.

As I mentioned in my own book, *What
God Says About Sex*, physical intimacy with
Lana was the most consistently exhilarating,
off-the-charts experience of my life! So
whether or not you choose to follow the path
I chose, I pray you'll make a commitment to
do *something* to protect your physical intimacy
and to keep it alive and active as long as you
both shall live. As the Bible says:

"Marriage should be honored by all, and the marriage bed kept pure..." (Hebrews 13:4a)

Honor your marriage and keep your marriage bed pure. Don't look for other ways to find physical pleasure. Look to your spouse and do whatever you can to nurture your relationship with them.

In the next chapter, the conclusion of this series!

Chapter 6

Believe it or not, all the tips I've shared with you up till now were just the preface, the introduction, to what I'd like to share with you today about how to have a stronger marriage.

When my friends asked me to talk about marriage at their wedding, and what made my marriage to Lana so special, I began to think through all the tips I've shared with you up to this point.

But as important as each of those tips are, I felt like the most important thought I could share with them was the one I'm going to share with you today. This idea focuses on just 3 words that really serve as the glue to hold all the other tips together.

Although there are a number of great phrases of 3 words I could have chosen (like "I love you," "I was wrong," "I am sorry," "I forgive you," or as one reader suggested,

"You're right, dear!"), I chose these 3 because they were 3 words our pastor shared with us at our wedding, and because they conclude a wonderful chapter in the Bible about how we relate to one another. I can honestly say these 3 words carried us through our 23 years together perhaps more than any other advice I've shared with you in this book.

You can read below the words I shared with my friends on their wedding day. You can also watch their wedding online on *The Ranch* website at the link below. It was a beautiful outdoor ceremony, complete with birds chirping and bales of hay on which the guests sat. The the ceremony's only about 30 minutes long, so feel free to take a look!

Here's the link to watch:
http://theranch.org/?attachment_id=17583

And here's the text of what I shared with this beautiful couple that day...

When I met with Korey and Makayla a few months ago to talk about their wedding, Makayla asked me to share some thoughts about what marriage means and what made my marriage to Lana work so well. She said she looked up to us and just wanted to hear from my heart.

So I'm going to tell you 3 short highlights, 3 little snippets from my life and my marriage that I hope will be helpful to you. Really it's summed up in 3 words; 3 words that I hope you'll remember today; 3 words that I hope you'll be able to put into practice in your own marriage.

You might think these 3 words are "I love you," but they're not. They're these:

"And be thankful."

There's a passage in the Bible that says many things about loving and caring for one another. The passage talks about all the things that we associate with love, such as:

"…clothe yourselves with compassion, kindness, humility, gentleness and patience. Bear with each other and forgive whatever grievances you may have against one another. Forgive as the Lord forgave you. And over all these virtues put on love, which binds them all together in perfect unity" (Colossians 3:12b-14).

These are all wonderful things. But then Paul goes on and adds these 3 words to all the rest, words that seem to go beyond even just loving each other. Paul says,

"And be thankful" *(Colossians 3:15b).*

Then he says it again in a lengthier way at the end of the whole passage:

"And whatever you do, whether in word or deed, do it all in the name of the Lord Jesus, giving thanks to God the Father" *(Colossians 3:17).*

I just want to tell you 3 little snapshots from my life about giving thanks to God for my wife.

On our wedding day, Lana and I wrote our own vows, like you've written your own vows. In my vows, I said to Lana: "Lana, you are a gift from God to me, and I plan to treat you as a gift." From that day on that's what I tried to do. That was the most amazing day to me, to be able to receive this gift from God and to be able to unwrap it over and over and over again, discovering layers of her that I had no idea about.

On our wedding day I said, "Thank You, Lord, and thank You, Lana, for saying 'Yes!' to marrying me."

Then I just kept saying that throughout my whole 23 years. When I would see how she raised our children, I would say, "Thank You, Lord, for this incredible mother of our children and thank you, Lana, for being a godly mother and wife." When I would see how she cooked meals for us, took care of us, edited my manuscripts for my ministry, I'd say, "Thank You, Lord, and thank you, Lana." Lana was a gift from God, and I was so thankful for her.

Our wedding day was 1 snapshot, but there was another snapshot I'd like to share with you, and you, Makayla, were actually very nearby. We were in Israel and Makayla and Jeanette had come with a few of us in our family to Israel and we were in the hotel at the Dead Sea. We had just had a beautiful night of worship, worshipping God in our room with our whole team. After everyone had left, Lana and I went out on the balcony on a beautiful night, and we had a wonderful, romantic, intimate night together. In the midst of that precious night, I just looked up to heaven and I said, "Thank You, Lord, and thank you, Lana." That was 1 of the most precious memories of my life. I can't count how many wonderful nights I've had like that with her, so often saying in the midst of them, "Thank You, Lord, and thank you, Lana."

Then there's a third moment I'd like to share with you, a little snapshot, and this was was just a couple years ago. We were in the car at Walmart, sitting in the parking lot after shopping one night. We were having a really hard conversation; one of those where you say, "Wow, this is hard." We didn't have many of those, but that night we were both feeling very passionate about what we felt and believed, and we just weren't on the same page.

The conversation had to do with what kind of treatment plan we were going to do for her cancer. I had one idea. She had another. And it just got more heated and more passionate. The doctors had told us no matter which path we chose, it wouldn't make any difference in the outcome, but we still wanted to try everything we could.

When were at the peak of that conversation, I had to stop and just say to myself, "Lana is a gift from God to me; she is not the problem here." Then rather than face each other and think that we were each other's problem, we had to put the problem to one side and turn shoulder to shoulder to work on it together.

I just had to back up and say, "Lana, you are a gift from God to me, and the reason I feel so passionate about this is because I just don't want to lose you. I want to do anything I can to keep you. And I want to remind you, in this conversation, in this heated moment, the only reason I feel so passionate about this is because I love you, so, so much."

That eased the tension. It changed the dynamics of the conversation.

In the end, it turned out the doctors were right and it wouldn't have mattered which plan we chose. Lana died just a few months later.

But I am so thankful that in those heated moments in the parking lot, I decided not to keep arguing over it, but rather to give thanks in all things and say, "Thank You, Lord, and thank you, Lana." She truly was a gift from God to me and I always wanted to treat her as a gift.

With all the other wonderful things you can do for your marriage, remember these 3 words because they can carry you through your whole life:

"And be thankful."

You understand what it means to forgive. You understand what it means to make a lifelong commitment. You understand love and graciousness and kindness and humility and being second and all those things.

I think you understand this, too, but I just want to highlight and emphasize—even beyond just loving each other, which is incredible—to be thankful.

"And be thankful."

"And be thankful."

"And be thankful."

And with those words, I married my friends to each other and I prayed that they, like you, would have a long, wonderful and thankful life together!

Will you pray with me?

Father, thank You for Your wisdom, which You've given to us through Your Word to help us to love one another in the best way possible. Help us to apply these words to all of our relationships so that we can love one other more fully and be more thankful in all that we do. Fill us with Your Spirit to do everything You've put on our hearts to do today and every day, from this day forward. We pray all this in the strong name of Jesus, who has the power to make all our relationships stronger, too. Amen.

Bonus Chapter - 12 Tips On Parenting!

As a father of 6 kids, I'm always glad to hear what others are doing to parent their kids. So when some friends of my college-age kids asked me what advice I would give them for raising kids of their own in the future, I put together this list of some of the best pieces of wisdom we gathered over the years that have worked well for us. I thought you might like to read it, too.

Since there are 12 tips and there are 12 months in the year, you might want to focus on trying 1 tip a each month. They're not in any particular order, so you can pick a tip for each month that seems most helpful to you at the time.

And even if you don't have kids in your life right now, maybe you know someone who does who might be interested in reading these tips. If so, please pass them along, as each tip includes a special word from God's Word. Even though I'm not a perfect father, I know Someone who is—and His wisdom can't be beat! With that disclaimer out of the way, here are my "12 Tips On Parenting."

1) Recognize that children are gifts from the Lord. Your attitude towards your children may be the single-most important item in your parenting toolbox. The Bible says that children are blessings, not burdens: "Blessed is the man whose quiver is full of them" (Psalm 127:5a).

You can check your attitude by asking what your heart feels when you hear of someone who already has 2 or 3 children and they tell you they're expecting a 3rd or 4th. Or 5th. Or 6th. Or 7th, etc. If your heart sinks with the addition of each child, you may secretly be viewing children as burdens, not blessings. If the same person had told you God had given them a 3rd or 4th car (or 5th or 6th or 7th, etc.), or a 3rd or 4th house (or 5th or 6th or 7th, etc.) and your attitude is like "Wow! That's incredible!" then you may want to re-think your attitude.

Children do take time and energy and attention, just as cars and houses do, and more children take more time and energy and attention, just as more cars and more houses do (just ask anyone who has more than one of any of these!) With great gifts comes great responsibility. But children, like any gifts from the Lord, are still gifts to be treasured, valued and held in the highest regard. Check your attitude, and remember that children really are gifts from the Lord.

2) Love your spouse. This tip may not seem like it has anything to do with parenting, but it's actually one of the best tips on this list! I have a plaque from my dad that says: "The most important thing a father can do for his children is to love their mother." My dad reminded me of this one day when I was feeling particularly inadequate about my parenting. He said, "You have no idea what you're doing for your children just by loving Lana." Looking back over the years, I'm sure he was right.

A genuine love between parents can do more for children than we can imagine. The Bible says, "Husbands, love your wives, just as Christ loved the church and gave Himself up for her… and the wife should respect her husband" (Ephesians 5:25 and 33b). Parents at odds cause children to take sides and respect only one or the other parent (or neither) and kids can play off that to try to get what they want. If you want your children to treat others with love and respect, then treat your husband or wife with love and respect (even if they don't do the same for you). Your children will be blessed as a result.

3) Realize that children take time. Children do take time, but they don't take time away from life. Children take time that enhances life. Trips to the zoo, trips to the beach, sitting down and playing games, setting limits on your workdays and Sundays and weekends so you can be with them, all take time away from other things you could be doing. But the return on your investment is so much greater, both in the moment and in the long run.

For Lana, when she decided to stay home from work so she could homeschool our kids and spend more time with them, it was costly on many levels: financially, personally and professionally. But she never felt like she was wasting her life by doing this, but investing her life. When she was facing death, way too young at the age of 48, she said she was thankful she had spent her time the way she did—with no regrets. Quality time is sometimes only possible because quantity time makes it so.

4) Let everyone work together to make the household work. One of the blessings for me of having a larger family has been to see how all the kids can work together to help keep our household running. Doing everything for our kids was never an option because we simply couldn't do it all. Responsibilities were given to each child as soon as they were able, from cooking and cleaning to dishes and laundry, from building and bookkeeping to yardwork and petkeeping.

The Bible says, "If you don't work, you don't eat" (2 Thessalonians 3:10, MSG). We never taught this in a mean-spirited way, but as a matter of getting things done more efficiently (or getting things done at all!) whether it was getting food to the table or chores finished on Saturday. For us, giving kids responsibility was both practical (for keeping our house running) and good training for their future.

5) Discipline in love, not in anger. Discipline is simply more effective when it is separated from anger. The Bible says, "Children, obey your parents in the Lord, for this is right…" (Ephesians 6:1) but that is quickly followed by these words: "Fathers, do not exasperate your children; instead, bring them up in the training and instruction of the Lord" (Ephesians 6:4).

I've found it best not to explode at my children, not because I don't want to, but because it's not useful. They can't hear you—or your love for them—when you're screaming. The times I most regret in my parenting are the times when I've disciplined in anger. But I've never regretted disciplining in love because that has set the stage for their future success in life. A simple tip: count to 10 before disciplining children. For teenagers, wait a week! (I'm serious!)

6) Pray for God to reveal the truth, even if it's painful to hear. A pastor's kid once said that it wasn't fair that his dad was a pastor, because God always seemed to tell his parents whenever he was doing something wrong. We really can pray that God will show us what's going on in our kids' lives, even when we can't see it ourselves. The Bible says, "He [God] gives wisdom to the wise and knowledge to the discerning. He reveals deep and hidden things; He knows what lies in darkness, and light dwells with Him" (Daniel 2:21b-22).

There have been times when I have prayed that God would show me if there's anything I should know about my kids so I can help them stay on the right path, even if it's something I didn't want to hear. I've been surprised when, soon after a prayer like this, God has revealed something to me—whether in a dream or a phone bill or an unexpected email—that was painful to hear but has opened the door to a conversation where I can help walk my kids through a difficult situation.

7) Love doesn't always say "Yes." A good parent wants to bless and please their children. But some parents say "Yes" to their kids' pleas solely to win their love and friendship, not because it's good or best for them.

There are times when your kids need a best friend and there are times when you can be one for them. But there are other times when they need you to be a parent, and only you can do that for them.

Some parents say "Yes" to all things in order to win their children's friendship. But a well-timed or well-reasoned "No" can be just as loving. The Bible says, "A word aptly spoken is like apples of gold in settings of silver" (Proverbs 25:11), which means that certain words we say are beautiful and perfectly fit for the occasion. While this applies to words of any type, it can especially apply to our yes's and no's.

8) Keep your words uplifting and encouraging. As parents, our words have an extra weight of authority. As such, we have to be extra careful with what we say, especially when it comes to criticism. Some people may say, "They have a face only a mother could love." But what if it's the mother who says, "You're ugly!" or "You can't sing!" or "You're no good at ___________ or ___________ or ___________!"

A good rule of thumb is to give at least 10

positive affirmations for every 1 correction, and then only if it's necessary for their benefit (for instance, to save them from embarrassment in public). Watch your words, especially your words of criticism. The Bible says, "Do not let any unwholesome talk come out of your mouths, but only what is helpful for building others up according to their needs, that it may benefit those who listen" (Ephesians 4:29).

9) Pray for your children starting before they're born, both privately and out loud. We've prayed for each of our children from the moment we knew they were in Lana's womb. We've prayed for their lives, their health, their faith, their futures, their callings, their spouses, their children and grandchildren and great grandchildren and so on! We've done this privately in our own quiet times, as well as out loud at nighttime when we tuck them into bed and kiss them good night.

I still do this even for my college-age kids when they're home, putting my hand on their heads and praying for them before they go to bed (or before I go to bed, which is more often the case these days!) It may seem awkward, but I believe in the power of prayer, plus I think it's important that our kids know that we're praying for them, as a matter of love and care. As the Bible says: "Therefore confess your sins to each other and pray for each other so that you may be healed. The prayer of a righteous man is powerful and effective" (James 5:16).

10) When your kids sin, love 'em more. Sometimes our kids do things that make us frustrated and make us want to pull back from them. But I've found that's the time I need to "love 'em more." Someone once asked the famous evangelist Billy Graham what he would do if he found out one of his children had sinned. He said, "Why, I'd love that one even more." It's not that Rev. Graham would love them more because of their sin, but because he knew that love is the best antidote to sin.

Our kids need love and acceptance, just like we do, and that's why they sometimes seek it out in the wrong places, just like we do. It's at times like these that they need to see our love and forgiveness for them more than ever, just as Jesus did for us when He died on the cross. As the Bible says, "God demonstrates His own love for us in this: While we were still sinners, Christ died for us" (Romans 5:8). When your kids hurt you or mistreat you or disappoint you, don't pull back. Do what Jesus did and "love 'em more."

11) Take breaks for rainbows. A life with kids is filled with interruptions. But don't take the interruptions as sidelines from life, but as one of the best parts of life itself. We have a painting in our home that says, "The work will wait while you show the children the rainbow, but the rainbow won't wait while you finish the work." Take advantage of those fleeting moments to enjoy your life with your children.

It's OK to stop and smell the roses. The Bible says, "Finally, brothers, whatever is true, whatever is noble, whatever is right, whatever is pure, whatever is lovely, whatever is admirable—if anything is excellent or praiseworthy—think about such things" (Philippians 4:8). When we moved to the country, Lana and I would take walks with our kids at sunset whenever we had the chance. There were always plenty of other things to do, but none of them so memorable to me as those sunset walks.

12) Let kids be kids, but don't let them be in danger. There's a fine line between letting kids be kids and letting them be in danger, because a lot of the things kids do can be dangerous! It's one thing if they want to let their hair grow out, but quite another if they want to hang out with dangerous people. It's one thing to let them be adventurous, but quite another to let them do something that's truly life threatening.

I've had to walk that fine line and have had multiple conversations with my kids about each of these things. And God is the one who has had to remind me multiple times to let my kids be kids, especially my teenagers. But I've also had to step in and say, "I'm glad to let you be a teenager, but I won't let you be in danger." That's just wisdom, and knowing which is which often comes only from God, who is happy to let us know the difference. If you're not sure what to do in a situation, ask God who is glad to pour out His wisdom on you. As the Bible says, "If any of you lacks wisdom, he should ask God, who gives generously to all without finding fault, and it will be given to him" (James 1:5).

Thanks for reading these 12 tips on parenting and thanks for passing them along to others who might benefit from reading them. Again, you might want to choose 1 tip each month to focus on with your kids this year or you might want to reread this message from time to time in the years ahead as your kids go through different stages of life. As I've been reminded often, none of us are perfect parents. But with God's help, we can keep trying to be the best that we can be.

May the Lord bless you as you seek to love and bless the children in your life!

In Christ's love,

Eric Elder

ABOUT THE AUTHOR

Eric Elder is an ordained pastor and the founder of a faith-boosting website called *The Ranch* at www.theranch.org. Eric was married to his precious wife, Lana, for 23 years until she passed on to be with the Lord in 2012. Together they've had 6 awesome children and a lifetime of wonderful memories.

If you enjoyed this book, you might also enjoy these other books by Eric and his wife:

Two Weeks With God
What God Says About Sex
Exodus: Lessons In Freedom
Jesus: Lessons In Love
Acts: Lessons In Faith
Nehemiah: Lessons In Rebuilding
Ephesians: Lessons In Grace
Israel: Lessons From The Holy Land
Israel For Kids: Lessons From The Holy Land
The Top 20 Passages In The Bible
Romans: Lessons In Renewing Your Mind
St. Nicholas: The Believer
and *Making The Most Of The Darkness*

To order or learn more, please visit:
WWW.INSPIRINGBOOKS.COM

Made in the USA
Monee, IL
13 September 2025

25617593R00049